I. Introduction

Congress greatly expanded the exercise of court-martial jurisdiction over civilians in 1950 with the enactment of the Uniform Code of Military Justice. Under this reform legislation, civilians serving with, employed by, or accompanying the armed forces overseas, and former servicemen charged with committing serious offenses while on active duty were made subject to court-martial jurisdiction. Within five years after enactment of the Code, however, the United States Supreme Court began to hold the provisions extending court-martial jurisdiction over civilians unconstitutional. The effect of these Supreme Court decisions was to limit the exercise of court-martial jurisdiction over civilians and former servicemen who committed offenses outside of the territorial jurisdiction of the United States.

Since these Supreme Court decisions were handed down during the late 1950s and early 1960s, the military authorities have been unable to exercise criminal jurisdiction over civilians accompanying the armed forces overseas or former servicemen who committed offenses overseas. Nor have the federal authorities been able to prosecute overseas offenders because the federal criminal code generally does not apply to crimes committed in foreign jurisdictions. The events at My Lai served to highlight the seriousness of the juris-

1

dictional void created by the Supreme Court decisions in this area. The inability to prosecute the soldiers involved at My Lai who had been discharged or released from active duty was widely publicized. As one former soldier indicated on network television, there was no need to fear prosecution for his actions at My Lai because he was no longer in the military service.[1]

The inability of either the military or federal authorities to prosecute former servicemen for criminal offenses committed while on active duty overseas is not new. The problem predates the Uniform Code of Military Justice as demonstrated by the case of In re Lo Dolce.[2] In Lo Dolce, American soldiers operating behind German lines in Italy were charged with murdering an American officer and placing his body in a lake where it was not discovered until 1950. The soldiers accused of the crime could not be prosecuted under the Articles of War because they had been discharged from the service.

In Hironimus v. Durant,[3] a WAC officer was convicted by general court-martial of the theft of jewelry from Kronberg Castle which belonged to Prince Wolfgang of Hesse and Prince August Wilhelm of Prussia. Her terminal leave was terminated only two days prior to the date she would have been released from active duty. Had she been released, it is doubtful if jurisdiction over her could have been obtained.

While overseas military commanders are responsible for

the prosecution of military offenders, they also are concerned with the conduct of civilians serving with, employed by or accompanying their commands. However, the lack of court-martial or federal jurisdiction over civilians accompanying the armed forces overseas prevents military commanders from initiating criminal proceedings when civilians with their commands have committed offenses. When no other criminal jurisdiction over civilians has been available, military authorities have resorted to the use of military commissions in times of war and occupation. The military commission, however, provides no criminal sanctions in time of peace.

The Criminal Justice Reform Act of 1975,[4] with its provisions for extraterritorial jurisdiction over civilians accompanying the armed forces, will provide a solution to the problems created by the Supreme Court decisions limiting court-martial jurisdiction. The passing of the Act will resolve many of the problems involved in the extending of federal jurisdiction over civilians and former servicemen who commit criminal offenses overseas. The Act, however, does not address the problem of determining what agency is responsible for prosecuting civilians accompanying the armed forces overseas in time of war or former servicemen charged with war crimes.

The armed forces should formulate a policy now for the

exercising of wartime court-martial jurisdiction over
civilians in conjunction with the proposed federal extraterritorial jurisdiction. Little time to devise a functional
policy will exist should there be a need for implementation.
Additionally, a policy concerning the prosecution of Americans
accused of war crimes is needed.

Before such policies can be determined, it is necessary
to understand the present extent of military jurisdiction
over civilians and the extent of military and federal extraterritorial jurisdiction under The Criminal Justice Reform
Act. To gain the required understanding, this article reviews
the process by which court-martial jurisdiction has been
limited in three different areas. These areas are the
jurisdiction over civilians accompanying the armed forces
overseas in time of peace, in time of war, and former servicemen charged with committing offenses while on active duty
overseas. Additionally, the judicially approved use of the
military commission is examined because of its possible
employment in occupied territory and as a means to prosecute
war crimes when no other adequate forum exists.

Military and federal extraterritorial jurisdiction after
passage of The Criminal Justice Reform Act is compared and
contrasted with a view toward the effect of the Act on
existing military jurisdiction. The areas of exclusive and
concurrent jurisdiction are delineated. A policy for the

armed forces is recommended in regard to the wartime prosecution of civilians when concurrent jurisdiction exists
under the new Act. Additionally, a policy concerning the
prosecution of Americans accused of war crimes is recommended.

In an effort to avoid a failure to obtain jurisdiction
over former servicemen because of subsequent unintended
interpretation of the extraterritorial provisions of the Act,
a change in the language of the provision is recommended.
Implementation of the changes and the policies recommended
will clarify when military jurisdiction exists over civilians
and former servicemen and will assist the wartime commander
in determining when to exercise court-martial jurisdiction
over civilians and when to seek prosecution under the new Act.

II. Refinement By the Judiciary

A. Former Servicemen

The reduction of court-martial jurisdiction over civilians
under the Uniform Code began in 1955 with the Supreme Court's
decision in United States ex rel. Toth v. Quarles.[5] In
Toth, the accused was honorably discharged from the United
States Air Force on December 8, 1952. Four months after his
discharge he was charged under Article 3(a) of the Uniform
Code of Military Justice[6] with the premeditated murder of a
Korean national and conspiracy to commit murder while on active

duty with the Air Force in Korea. Article 3(a) of the Code provided court-martial jurisdiction over former servicemen for certain serious offenses committed while on active duty if no federal or state jurisdiction existed.

He subsequently was arrested by Air Force police at his place of employment in Pittsburgh and returned to Korea. A petition for habeas corpus was then filed in his behalf and the Supreme Court granted certiorari after relief was denied by the Court of Appeals.

The Government contended that Article 3(a) was a valid exercise of the power granted Congress by Article I, § 8, clause 14 of the Constitution "To make Rules for the Government and Regulation of the land and naval Forces," as supported by the Necessary and Proper clause.[7] The Court, however, found that Article I restricted court-martial jurisdiction to only those "actually members or part of the armed forces" and that any such extension of court-martial jurisdiction to former servicemen would be an encroachment on the jurisdiction of the Article III courts.[8] The Court then held that Congress could not subject civilians like Toth to trial by court-martial.[9]

B. Peacetime Jurisdiction over Civilians Overseas

Two years later the Supreme Court further reduced the jurisdiction of courts-martial over civilians with its decision in the case of Reid v. Covert.[10] The decision resulted from the general courts-martial convictions of two dependent wives of murdering their servicemen husbands in England and Japan.[11] Jurisdiction in both of these courts-martial was asserted under Article 2(11) of the Code which in part provided for court-martial jurisdiction over a person accompanying the armed forces outside of the United States.[12] The Court was unable to enter a majority opinion, but rather issued three opinions disapproving court-martial jurisdiction in these cases.

The opinion of Justice Black, in which three other Justices joined, concluded that dependents accompanying a serviceman abroad are not members of the "land and naval Forces" and, therefore, they do not lose their civilian status and their right to trial by a civilian forum.[13] Justice Frankfurter, concurring, concluded that in view of the protections of Article III and the Fifth and Sixth Amendments, Article I does not justify "the exercise of court-martial jurisdiction over civilian dependents in time of peace."[14] Justice Harlan also concurred in the narrow result that Article 2(11) could not be constitutionally applied in a capital case to the court-martial of civilian dependents of servicemen overseas in peacetime.[15]

In 1960 the Supreme Court examined the remaining portion of Article 2(11) in the companion cases of Kinsella v. United States ex rel. Singleton,[16] Grisham v. Hagan,[17] and McElroy v.

United States ex rel. Guagliardo.[18] In Singleton, the Court
was presented with the direct appeal of a petition for habeas
corpus on behalf of Mrs. Joanna S. Dial who had been convicted along with her soldier husband by a general court-
martial in Germany of the voluntary manslaughter of one of
her children. The Court concluded that inasmuch as it
previously had held in the Covert decision that the Necessary
and Proper Clause cannot expand Clause 14 so as to include
prosecution of civilian dependents for capital crimes, neither
can it expand Clause 14 to include their prosecution for non-
capital offenses.[19] The Court held that Mrs. Dial was pro-
tected by the provisions of Article III and the Fifth and
Sixth Amendments and that, therefore, she could not be
constitutionally prosecuted by court-martial.[20]

In Grisham v. Hagan[21] the Court considered the habeas
corpus petition of a civilian employed by the Army in France
who had been charged with premeditated murder. The accused
was convicted by a general court-martial of the lesser included offense of unpremeditated murder. The Court held that
this case was also controlled by the Covert decision inasmuch
as there was no distinction between a civilian employee
charged with a capital offense and a civilian dependent
charged with a capital offense.[22]

The Court completed the nullification of Article 2(11)
by considering its applicability to non-capital offenses

committed by civilian employees overseas in McElroy v. United States ex rel. Guagliardo[23] and Wilson v. Bohlender.[24] The Court found that these cases were controlled by the decisions in Singleton and Hagan and, therefore, held that the trial by court-martial of such civilian employees for noncapital offenses was unconstitutional.[25] The entire line of Supreme Court decisions concerning military jurisdiction over civilians demonstrates that the subjecting of civilians to court-martial jurisdiction in peacetime was beyond the constitutional power of Congress to make rules for the regulation of the armed forces.

C. Wartime Jurisdiction Over Civilians

Judicial review of jurisdiction over civilians "in time of war" was provided by the United States Court of Military Appeals in the case of United States v. Averette[26] decided in April 1970. This decision reduced military jurisdiction under Article 2(10) of the Code which specifically provides for time of war jurisdiction over "persons serving with or accompanying an armed force in the field."[27] In Averette, the accused was a civilian employee of an Army contractor in Vietnam. He was convicted by a general court-martial at Long Binh, Vietnam, of conspiracy to commit larceny and attempted larceny of 36,000 United States Government-owned batteries. The court, after recognizing the delicacy of

9

extending court-martial jurisdiction over civilians, concluded that the words "in time of war" meant, for the purposes of Article 2(10) of the Code, "a war formally declared by Congress."[28] The court noted that the Vietnam conflict was "a major military action,"[29] but that nothing short of a formal declaration of war would satisfy the definition of war, "at least in the sensitive area of subjecting civilians to military jurisdiction."[30]

The definition of "in time of war" often has depended on the purpose for which the term was used and what jurisdiction was making the determination. Areas of the law where a definition of "in time of war" has been needed include litigation involving life insurance and the seizure and destruction of shipping.[31] The legislative history of the Code reveals that there was no discussion of the meaning of the phrase "in time of war" in either the House or Senate Committee reports, nor was there any discussion concerning the same during Congressional debate.[32] The court in Averette acknowledged that it previously had found the Korean conflict to be a war in connection with the severity of the sentence that could be imposed for certain offenses in time of war.[33] The court also noted that in United States v. Anderson[34] the Vietnam conflict had been found to be "in time of war" for the purposes of suspending the statute of limitations for desertion and absence without leave offenses. The court distinguished these cases, however, as involving military

personnel and military offenses, while the Averette decision

involved "the constitutionally delicate question of military

jurisdiction over civilians."[35]

The court thereafter relied upon Averette in the case

of Zamora v. Woodson[36] decided in May 1970. Zamora was

charged with 56 specifications alleging violations of a

general regulation concerning the purchase of money orders in

Vietnam. Jurisdiction was premised on Zamora's status as

"a United States civilian, a person serving with or accompanying

the Armed Forces in the field in time of war."[37] Zamora filed

with the Court of Military Appeals an "Appeal from Denial of

Extraordinary Relief"[38] after a military trial judge had denied

his requested relief. The court, addressing only the one

issue, held that the Averette decision controlled in this

case and dismissed the charge and specifications pending

against Zamora.[39]

The United States Court of Claims also applied Averette

in Robb v. United States.[40] In Robb the administratrix of

Robert J. Poor, a deceased civilian employee of the United

States Navy in Vietnam, attempted to recover a $5,000 fine

imposed upon Poor as the result of a 1968 conviction by

general court-martial of using military postal facilities to

import diamonds into Vietnam and of postal money order

violations. This conviction was affirmed by the Navy Board of

Review and Poor did not petition the United States Court of Military Appeals. The Court of Claims, acknowledging the special competence of the Court of Military Appeals, specifically followed the Averette decision and held that the phrase "in time of war" in Article 2(10) refers to a state of war formally declared by Congress and that without such a declaration a court-martial has no jurisdiction over a civilian who is "serving with or accompanying an armed force in the field."[41] The Court of Claims found the court-martial that convicted Poor had no jurisdiction over him and allowed the plaintiff to recover the fine imposed on Poor.[42]

Prior to Averette, jurisdiction under Article 2(10) had been challenged in Latney v. Ignatius.[43] Latney involved the appeal of a United States District Court's dismissal of a petition for writ of habeas corpus which eventually was decided in the context of to whom Article 2(10) applied, rather than the nature of the conflict to which it applied. Latney, an Able-bodied seaman of the United States Merchant Marine, was convicted by a general court-martial in February 1968 of the unpremeditated murder of another American merchant seaman in a bar in DaNang, South Vietnam. The court, recognizing "the spirit of O'Callahan,[44] and of the other Supreme Court precedents there reviewed"[45] determined that Article 2(10) is not to be viewed so expansively as to reach a civilian seaman employed by a civilian shipping company in no closer proximity to the armed forces than being in port for a short period while still living on his ship under the discipline of his civilian captain.[46]

While the Supreme Court has not had occasion to rule on the application of the Uniform Code to civilians during a time of war, the Court of Military Appeals has now limited court-martial jurisdiction over civilians to only a time of declared war. The limitation has the effect of placing civilians serving with or accompanying our military forces in combat areas in the same category as they would be in a peacetime environment if no declaration of war exists. The net result of Averette and the Supreme Court decisions dealing with civilians accompanying the armed forces in time of peace is a substantial narrowing of the Code's provisions for extending a form of extraterritorial jurisdiction over American civilians in close proximity to our armed forces overseas.

III. The Current Status of Military Jurisdiction Over Civilians Overseas

The current state of the law in the area of military jurisdiction over civilians must be understood before solutions can be devised. Presently, military jurisdiction over civilians can potentially be exercised by means of trial by court-martial in time of declared war and trial by military commission. Court-martial jurisdiction is created by statute while the source of military commission jurisdiction is derived from the inherent war-making powers of the Government.

A. Violations of the Code

Court-martial jurisdiction over civilians under the Code historically may be viewed as falling into three categories. These are jurisdiction over civilians accompanying the armed forces overseas during peacetime, jurisdiction over former servicemen, and jurisdiction over civilians in time of war.

1. Article 2(11)--Jurisdiction in Time of Peace

The decisions of the Supreme Court in Covert and in the subsequent cases hold that Article 2(11) of the Code can no longer constitutionally be applied to obtain court-martial jurisdiction over civilian dependents or civilians serving with, employed by, or accompanying the armed forces outside the United States. Unless an offense committed by such a person is one of those for which there presently exists extraterritorial federal jurisdiction, no jurisdiction by any court in the United States will lie. The offender will either be prosecuted by another nation that can exert jurisdiction or will escape prosecution altogether.

2. Article 3(a)--Jurisdiction over Former Servicemen

The decision of the Supreme Court in Toth also leaves the

Executive Branch without the means to prosecute former service personnel for most violations of the Code committed while on active duty in a foreign jurisdiction. Prosecution would be possible only if the offense also constituted a violation of the United States Code that applied extra-territorially. Another possibility would be where the offense constitutes a war crime and jurisdiction can be found under Article 18 of the Code or in a military commission.

3. Article 2(10)--Jurisdiction in Time of War

The court-martial jurisdiction of persons serving with or accompanying an armed force in the field pursuant to Article 2(10) has been restricted in regard to what constitutes a "time of war" by the Averette decision. Nevertheless, a close scrutiny of the cases dealing with this provision of the Code and prior Supreme Court cases dealing with Article 2(11) leads to a reasonable conclusion that such jurisdiction continues to exist during a war formally declared by Congress. The Court of Military Appeals in Averette reviewed all of the important Supreme Court decisions disapproving the trial by court-martial of persons not members of the armed forces. The court reasoned that since

> all of these decisions covered offenses occurring in periods other than in time of war, they do not constitute authority that even in time of declared war courts-martial have no jurisdiction to try those who are not members of the armed forces, regardless of the connection between their offenses and the objectives of military discipline.[47]

The court further found nothing in the O'Callahan opinion from which to conclude that "a civilian accompanying the armed forces in the field in time of a declared war is invulnerable to trial by military courts"[48] since the decision involved an active duty serviceman. The court also noted that the Latney decision was based primarily on the absence of a connection between the accused and the armed forces rather than on whether a time of war existed.[49]

The court, however, while finding no authority in previous cases to preclude wartime court-martial jurisdiction, specifically refused to express an opinion on the constitutional issue of whether Congress could provide for court-martial jurisdiction over civilians accompanying the armed forces in the field in time of declared war.[50]

The Averette decision in effect only postponed resolving the issue of to what extent Congress can provide court-martial jurisdiction over civilians in time of war. Judicial approval of the authority of Congress to provide wartime court-martial jurisdiction over civilians must be found in earlier decisions. The Supreme Court in Covert noted that there previously had been a number of federal court decisions upholding the military trial of civilians performing services for the armed forces in the field during time of war and that the justification for such jurisdiction rests on the Government's "war powers."[51] The Supreme Court went on to state that

> in the face of an actively hostile enemy, military
> commanders necessarily have broad power over persons on
> the battlefront. From a time prior to the adoption of
> the Constitution the extraordinary circumstances present
> in an area of actual fighting have been considered
> sufficient to permit punishment of some civilians in
> that area by military courts under military rules.[52]

In a footnote to the decision the Court stated its belief "that

Art. 2(10) sets forth the maximum historically recognized

extent of military jurisdiction over civilians under the

concept of 'in the field'."[53] The Court in McElroy dis-

tinguished the military trials of civilians during the Rev-

olutionary Period because they occurred during a period of

war.[54]

Even though the Supreme Court has not reviewed a

conviction under Article 2(10), the necessity of that

provision of the Code has been recognized. The comments of

the Court in Covert and McElroy and the precedents established

by the many decisions of the lower federal courts in upholding

convictions of civilians in the field in time of war prior to

the existence of the Code[55] is a definite indication that

Article 2(10) court-martial jurisdiction continues to exist

in time of declared war.

The distinction between time of peace and time of war

made by the Supreme Court in Covert and McElroy confirms the

opinion of the Court of Military Appeals that these decisions were not meant to effect the jurisdiction of courts-martial under Article 2(10). The fact that Article 2(10) has neither expressly been overruled nor subjected to judicial criticism in other opinions attests to its continuing validity as a necessary exercise of Congressional war powers authority.

B. Military Commission--The Common-law War Court

In time of war civilians can be tried by court-martial or military commission. Civilians also can be tried by military commissions in areas under military occupation. Although the use of the military commission is limited to time of war or occupation, it does provide an alternate source of criminal jurisdiction over civilians overseas. Use of the military commission by the United States began in 1847 when American military forces occupied portions of the territory of Mexico. At that time various military commanders convened military commissions to try individuals charged with offenses that generally could have been tried in the civil courts had they been functioning.[56] The military commission has continued to be recognized and sanctioned by the judiciary from the time of its earliest use through World War II and the occupations that followed.

Authority for the establishment of the military commission derives from the war powers vested in Congress by Article I, § 8, clause 1 and clauses 11 through 16,[57] and by Article I, § 8, clause 10,[58] which confers upon Congress the power to "define and punish--Offenses against the Law of Nations." This authority also is considered to derive from the power of the President as Commander-in-Chief of the Nation's armed forces as provided by Article II, § 2, clause 1.[59] The authority is defined as

> the same as the authority for the making and waging of war and for the exercise of military government and martial law. The commission is simply an instrumentality for the more efficient execution of the war powers vested in Congress and the power vested in the President as Commander-in-chief in war.[60]

While Congress has on occasion provided for the trial of certain offenses by military commission, the President and subordinate military commanders usually have been the authority for the establishment of such tribunals. Because the military commission has no statutory basis it has been defined by a Judge Advocate General of the Army as "our common-law war court."[61]

The trial of violators of the law of war and the trial of those not subject to the Articles of War or the Uniform Code of Military Justice in areas where the civil courts were not functioning have been the two primary uses of military commissions.

1. Violations of the Law of War
By Enemy Belligerents

The Supreme Court approved the use of military commissions to try and punish enemy belligerents charged with violations of the law of war during World War II in Ex parte Quirin[62] and In re Yamashita.[63] Ex parte Quirin arose as the result of the apprehension of the petitioners after they had entered this country from German submarines at Long Island, New York, and Ponte Vedra Beach, Florida, during June 1942. Each of the petitioners had been born in Germany, but had lived in the United States. All of the petitioners were citizens of the German Reich except one who contended that he was a naturalized citizen of the United States. Upon landing the petitioners, who were carrying explosives and incendiary devices, buried their German Marine Infantry uniforms and proceeded to various points within this country before they were subsequently apprehended by federal agents.

The President appointed a military commission to try the petitioners for offenses against the law of war and the Articles of War in conjunction with a proclamation of the same date which provided that such offenders of the law of war would be subject to the jurisdiction of military tribunals. The proclamation also denied those persons access to the civilian courts. The petitioners contended that the President was without the authority to order their trial by military tribunal and that they were entitled to trial in the civilian courts inasmuch as these courts were functioning in New York and Florida at that time.

In denying the petitioners relief, the Court noted that the Constitution conferred upon Congress the power to "define

and punish...offenses against the Law of Nations"[64] and that
Congress had recognized the military commission appointed by
military command by the authorization of such tribunals in
the Articles of War.[65] In addition, the Court noted that it
had "from the very beginning of its history" recognized and
applied the law of war as a part of the law of nations.[66]

For these reasons, the Supreme Court found that the
Constitution and its Amendments did not preclude trial by
military commission of any person, whether alien or citizen,
who had "violated the law of war applicable to enemies."[67]
Furthermore, the Court found that the petitioners were not
entitled to a jury trial because of the nature of their offenses
and not because of their status as aliens.[68] The Court held
that the acts of the petitioners constituted offenses against
the law of war which could constitutionally be tried by
military commission.[69] The Court, however, refused to define
the ultimate boundaries of the jurisdiction of military
commissions.[70]

The second case, In re Yamashita,[71] arose at the conclusion of hostilities in World War II. General Yamashita,
prior to his surrender on September 3, 1945, had been the
Commanding General of the Fourteenth Army Group of the
Imperial Japanese Army in the Philippine Islands. On
September 25, 1945, he was served with charges alleging his
violation of the law of war in that while acting as a
commander of Japanese armed forces in the Philippine Islands

21

he "unlawfully disregarded and failed to discharge his duty as (a) commander to control the operations of the members of his command, permitting them to commit brutal attrocities...."[72] Yamashita was tried by military commission of five Army officers appointed by the Commanding General of the United States Army Forces, Western Pacific, and on December 7, 1945, he was found guilty as charged and sentenced to death. General Yamashita applied to the Supreme Court of the Commonwealth of the Philippines for writs of habeas corpus and prohibition. After being denied relief he petitioned the United States Supreme Court for review contending that a military commission could not be lawfully convened after cessation of hostilities and that the authorized procedure of the commission deprived him of a fair trial in violation of the due process clause of the Fifth Amendment.[73]

The Court found that military commissions are courts whose rulings and judgments are subject to review only by the military authorities.[74] Therefore it considered only the lawful power of the military commission to try the petitioner for the charged offense.[75] The Court then reaffirmed the principle that a military commission appointed by a military command had been recognized by Congress as an appropriate tribunal for the trial of violations of the law of war.[76] As to the first contention, the Court determined that the power of military tribunals to try violations of the law of war does not cease to exist until such time as peace has been proclaimed by the "political branch of the government."[77] The Court observed that many offenders cannot be apprehended and held to account for their actions until hostilities have ceased.[78]

In addition, Yamashita contended that the commission admitted, over objection, opinion evidence, hearsay, and depositions contrary to the Articles of War. The Court held that petitioner as an enemy combatant was not subject to the Articles of War and the commission was not obligated to follow the rules of evidence and procedure provided by the Articles.[79] The Court found the procedure of the commission to be that determined as appropriate by the convening military command.[80]

In addition to the Court's decision in Quirin and Yamashita, the decision of Johnson v. Eisentrager,[81] decided in 1950, also recognized the "well-established" jurisdiction of military commissions to punish those guilty of offenses against the law of war.[82] In Eisentrager, the petitioners were German nationals convicted by an American military commission in China of violating the laws of war by engaging in continued military activity against the United States after the surrender of Germany.[83] Subsequent to conviction, the petitioners were repatriated to Germany to serve their sentences. The Court found no right on their part to the writ of habeas corpus inasmuch as they were enemy aliens who had not been within the territorial jurisdiction of the United States at any relevant time during their captivity.[84] The

Quirin, Yamashita and Eisentrager decisions are significant
primarily because they clearly establish that both aliens and
citizens who violate the law of war as enemy belligerents or
combatants are constitutionally subject to trial by military
commission.

2. Commission Jurisdiction Over Civilians

Clearly, enemy belligerents and combatants can be tried
by military commissions for violations of the law of war. The
use of the military commission to try civilians who are not
considered belligerents is a more difficult question. Outside
of the area of martial law, the United States has used the
commission primarily in furtherance of its duties as the
governing power in occupied territory. The Supreme Court
reviewed the constitutionality of military commission
jurisdiction over civilians in an occupied area in the post
World War II decision of Madsen v. Kinsella.[85]

In Madsen, the accused, a native-born citizen of the
United States, entered the American Zone of Occupied
Germany in 1947 as the dependent wife of an Air Force officer.
In October 1949 she was arrested and charged with the murder
of her husband in violation of the German Criminal Code. The
following February she was tried and convicted of the charges
by The United States Court of the Allied High Commission for
Germany, Fourth Judicial District. The conviction was affirmed
by the Court of Appeals of the United States Courts of the

Allied High Commission for Germany. These courts were composed

of civilians who were appointed by a United States Military

Governor. She subsequently petitioned for a writ of habeas

corpus and after relief was denied by the lower courts,

the Supreme Court granted certiorari.

The Supreme Court found that because Congress had not

attempted to limit the President's power, his authority as

Commander-in-Chief "appears" to include the power in time of

war to establish and determine the jurisdiction and procedure

of military commissions and other tribunals of like nature

in territory occupied by the armed forces of the United

States.[86] The Court further noted that the authority can

extend beyond the termination of actual hostilities because

the President also has the additional responsibility of

governing any territory occupied by our forces[87] and because

the "law of war" includes the power and duties of an occupying

force.[88] This obligation is consistent with Article 43 of the

Hague Convention No IV[89] which provides that the occupying

power is to take the necessary measures to restore public order

and safety.

The Court found the Military Government Courts to be a

part of the military government established by the President

as Commander-in-Chief. As occupation courts in the nature of

military commissions, they derived their authority from the

President[90] and, therefore, had jurisdiction to try the

petitioner.[91]

25

Because the Court decided Madsen five years prior to the decision in Covert, it was assumed that a general court-martial would also have had jurisdiction over Mrs. Madsen pursuant to a provision of the Articles of War similar to Article 2(11) of the Code.[92] Although the dissenting opinion in Covert addresses the similarity of the status of the accused and offenses in the two cases,[93] the majority opinion only notes that for other than those subject to the Code, the civilian courts normally have the power to try persons charged with crimes against the United States.[94] The opinion contrasts the jurisdiction of military courts with that of the civilian courts by defining "the jurisdiction of military tribunals as a very limited and extraordinary jurisdiction" derived from Article I, § 8, which is only a narrow exception to the preferred civil trial.[95]

The language of the Covert opinion can lead to a questioning of the continuing validity of Madsen inasmuch as both cases concerned military jurisdiction over United States civilians. The defendents in both Madsen and Covert were dependent wives of servicemen. The primary difference between the two cases was the status of the territory where the military forces were located. However, the Court in a footnote to the Covert decision distinguished Madsen because it concerned a trial in an occupied territory which was being governed by our military forces.[96] The footnote further acknowledged that in occupied territory a military commander can establish military or civilian commissions with jurisdiction over everyone within the area of occupation.[97]

Further Supreme Court recognition of the jurisdiction of military commissions in occupied territory was provided by the decision of Wilson v. Bohlender.[98] In Wilson, the petitioner was a civilian employee of the Army in Berlin who had been convicted by a general court-martial of sodomy. Jurisdiction had been invoked under Article 2(11) of the Code. The petitioner challenged the Article 2(11) jurisdiction as being unconstitutional. The Government responded by contending that he was subject to military government jurisdiction because the offense occurred in the United States Area of Control in West Berlin. The Court, as indicated in a footnote to the decision, rejected the contention because this theory of jurisdiction had not been relied upon by the court-martial or the Court of Military Appeals.[99] Thus as late as 1957 the Supreme Court recognized the jurisdiction of military commissions over all persons in occupied territory and at least noted the existence of such jurisdiction in the 1960 Wilson decision.

In 1967 the jurisdiction of military commissions was recognized by the United States Court of Appeals for the District of Columbia. In Rose v. McNamara,[100] a naturalized United States citizen residing on Okinawa who was the proprietress of a local business known as the Tea House August

Moon, was convicted by a jury in a court of the civil administration of evading taxes imposed by the Ryukyuan legislature. A local appellate court affirmed the conviction and Rose brought suit in United States District Court seeking a declaratory judgment that her conviction was a nullity. After being denied relief in that court she appealed.

The Court of Appeals noted that the Ryukyu Islands, which included Okinawa, had been taken and occupied by United States armed forces in the last days of World War II. The Treaty of Peace between Japan and the Allied Powers provided that the United States would exercise all power of administration, legislation and jurisdiction over this territory.[101] Pursuant to the treaty, President Eisenhower issued an executive order providing for the government of the Ryukyus. This order provided for a civil administration with a system of trial and appellate courts with both civil and criminal jurisdiction over American citizens. Because of concern with the Covert decision, a 1963 ordinance of the civil administration provided for grand jury indictment and petit jury trial for criminal defendants in these courts.[102]

The Court of Appeals affirmed the District Court in denying relief by noting that the Supreme Court's decision in Madsen "recognized an extensive power in the President, absent Congressional provision, to set up special tribunals in occupied foreign lands to try American citizens for crime."[103]

The Court of Appeals decision noted that the Supreme Court had previously held this power could survive the cessation of hostilities and even a treaty of peace if necessary for "the occupying power to discharge its responsibilities."[104]

It is reasonable to assume from Madsen and Rose and the comments of the Supreme Court in the Wilson decision that the military commission as established by Congress or by the authority of the President as Commander-in-Chief continues to exist as a constitutional tribunal. The jurisdiction of the military commission has been approved by the Supreme Court over all persons in the territory of a belligerent occupied by United States armed forces, either during hostilities or during a subsequent occupation.

3. War Crimes By Persons With the Armed Forces

Clearly military commission jurisdiction exists over all persons in occupied territory and over all persons who violate the law of war as enemy belligerents or combatants. A more difficult question is raised by violations of the law of war by those serving with the armed forces of the United States. There exists very little legal precedent in this area, primarily because the vast majority of offenses that could be considered war crimes have been prosecuted under the Articles of War or the Uniform Code of Military Justice. For example, Lieutenant Calley could have been charged with war crimes, but was prosecuted instead for violations of the punitive articles

of the Code.[105] However, since <u>Toth</u>, prosecution under the
punitive articles of the Code is no longer possible once a
serviceman is discharged or released from active duty.
Additionally, under <u>Averette</u>, a civilian serving with the armed
forces in combat can be prosecuted for a violation of the
punitive articles only if the conflict constitutes a declared
war. Jurisdiction must, therefore, be found elsewhere for
war crimes committed by those not subject to the Code.

The duty to prosecute military personnel and United
States citizens serving with the armed forces for violations
of the law of war long has been recognized and sanctioned by
the courts. Colonel Winthrop, as early as 1886, listed
officers and soldiers of the army, or persons serving with it
in the field as persons subject to prosecution for violations
of the law of war.[106] More recently, Congress recognized
trial by court-martial and military commission for violations
of the law of war by including Articles 18[107] and 21[108] in
the Uniform Code.

International obligations also impose a duty upon the
Government to prosecute personnel serving with the armed
forces for war crimes. Each of the four Geneva Conventions
for the Protection of War Victims of 12 August 1949[109] require
the High Contracting Parties to enact legislation necessary to
provide effective penal sanctions for persons who have committed,
or ordered committed, grave breaches of the Conventions.[110]

Additionally, each High Contracting Party is required to bring such persons before its own courts or to hand such persons over to another High Contracting Party for trial.[111] The United Nations Economic and Social Council Resolution of 18 May 1973[112] requires war crimes and crimes against humanity to be investigated and those accused of such acts to be subject to trial. The Resolution also calls for international cooperation in bringing offenders to justice and prohibits legislation or other action which is prejudicial to the imposed obligations. If the United States is to honor these international obligations, the means to prosecute violators of the law of war within the armed forces must be developed.

Another factor to be considered in the case of grave breaches of the Geneva Conventions is that violators are subject to prosecution before the courts of any High Contracting Party regardless of nationality.[113] Failure to take action to prosecute offenders within the military forces invites other nations who are parties to the Conventions to search for, apprehend, and try those suspected of grave breaches should the opportunity arise.

Persons serving with the armed forces who violate the laws of war fall into two classes. The first class consists of persons subject to the Uniform Code of Military Justice at the time of the offense and at the time of trial. The second

31

class consists of persons not subject to the Code at any time and persons subject to the Code at the time of the offense but not at the time of trial.

Members of the first class always would be subject to trial by court-martial. As a practical matter, virtually any violation of the law of war also would constitute a violation of one of the punitive articles of the Code. If for some reason the violation could not be charged as an offense under one of the punitive articles, trial by general court-martial under Article 18 of the Code would be available. The pertinent portion of Article 18 provides that "(g)eneral courts-martial also have jurisdiction to try any person who by the law of war is subject to trial by military tribunal and may adjudge any punishment permitted by the law of war."[114] The use of Article 18 jurisdiction would ensure an accused the same protections, both constitutional and statutory, that exist for one accused of any offense under the Code, and it is difficult to foresee any valid claims of prejudice to the rights of the accused in such a proceeding. Therefore, whether a person subject to the Code is tried on a charge of violating one of the punitive articles or under Article 18 would make little difference in the procedure used by the court-martial.

Prosecution of persons within the second class of offenders presents a complex situation. Trial by court-martial for a violation of the punitive articles of the Code is not available either because the accused was not subject to the Code when the offense was committed or because the accused is no longer subject to the Code. An example of a person not subject to the Code would be a civilian accompanying the armed forces in the field during combat operations not amounting to a declared war, who commits an act that constitutes both a violation of the law of war and of the punitive articles of the Code. Because the Averette decision narrowed the jurisdiction of the Code under Article 2(10) to times of declared war, the accused could not be charged with the violation of a punitive article. Yet, international law may consider the conflict a war. International agreements such as the Geneva Conventions recognize hostilities that are not the result of a formal declaration of war as conflicts to which the laws of war apply.[115] To view such conflicts otherwise would allow nations to avoid their international obligations and the laws of war merely by refusing to declare war or to acknowledge a state of war.

The situation of an offender no longer being subject to the Code occurs where a serviceman has committed an offense, but is discharged from the service or is released from active duty before charges are preferred against him. Since Toth, the discharge or separation from active duty precludes jurisdiction under the Code for a violation of the punitive articles.

Jurisdiction over war crimes must be sought elsewhere when

33

the offense is not a violation of the punitive articles of the Code or when the offender is not subject to the Code. Unless the war crime can be prosecuted in the federal courts, the military commission is the only other source of jurisdiction. Military commissions have been recognized as proper tribunals for the trial of military members and persons accompanying the military forces in time of war since the Civil War.[116]

The use of the military commission to try American citizens for a violation of the law of war has been approved by the courts. While this is true, the courts have not had occasion to consider a case involving the prosecution of a member of the United States military forces for a war crime where the victim was an enemy belligerent or foreign national. In the Quirin decision, one of the German sabatours claimed to be a United States citizen. The Supreme Court, however, found it unnecessary to resolve the issue of citizenship because as an unlawful belligerent he was in violation of the law of war.[117] His United States citizenship did not preclude military commission jurisdiction.[118]

In 1956 the United States Court of Appeals for the Tenth Circuit handed down a similar decision in the case of Colepaugh v. Louney.[119] In Colepaugh, a United States citizen secretly entered the country from a German submarine. He came ashore without a uniform and while carrying a weapon and espionage paraphenalia. He subsequently was apprehended and tried and convicted by a military commission. The Court of Appeals found that Colepaugh's United States citizenship did not divest the military commission of its jurisdiction over him nor did it "confer upon him any constitutional rights not accorded any other belligerent under the laws of war."[120]

In both Quirin and Colepaugh the federal courts approved military commission jurisdiction over United States citizens. However, the defendants in these cases were acting as enemy belligerents. While it can be argued that the Toth decision would preclude jurisdiction by a military commission as well as by court-martial, the two types of jurisdiction can be distinguished. Toth dealt only with the issue of whether the Congress in furtherance of its constitutional power "to make Rules for the Government and Regulation of the land and naval Forces,"[121] could extend court-martial jurisdiction to former servicemen for crimes committed while on active duty. The decision dealt only with jurisdiction pursuant to the Uniform Code of Military Justice and did not discuss common-law military commission jurisdiction. The decision did cite, however, Quirin and Yamashita as authority for the proposition that the jurisdiction of the Code over Toth could not be sustained by the war powers of Congress or the power of Congress to punish "Offenses against the Law of Nations."[122] Madsen was not cited in Toth although the earlier decision affirmed the jurisdiction of a tribunal in the nature of a military commission over a United States citizen who was not acting for a belligerent.

The Toth decision therefore must be viewed narrowly as applying only to violations of the punitive articles of the Code and not to violations that constitute war crimes. There is nothing in Toth or the series of Supreme Court decisions that followed concerning court-martial jurisdiction that would indicate a limiting of military commission jurisdiction.

The most difficult aspect of using the military commission to try American citizens for war crimes is that a decision by the Executive Branch is required to initiate the proceedings. The act of convening a military commission would be viewed by the public, both here and abroad, as tantamount to admitting that United States personnel have committed war crimes. The charging of a serviceman with a war crime also can result in the arousing of public sympathy for the person charged. This is particularly true where the victims are foreign nationals or enemy belligerents. The public support that developed for Lieutenant Calley after charges arising out of My Lai were preferred against him provides an example of such public sympathy and support for a defendant. The factor of possible public support for the defendant and the requirement that the Government, as the prosecution, produce the evidence of war crimes by Americans results in a reluctance to convene military commissions.

Congress, by including Article 18 in the Code provided a second source of jurisdiction over war crimes. Article 18 provides for general court-martial jurisdiction over all persons who are subject by the law of war to trial by military tribunal. Thus, Congress created a broad court-martial jurisdiction over war crimes. Included within the jurisdiction are not only American military personnel, but also the military personnel of any belligerent and the civilian citizens of all nations during time of armed conflict or military occupation.

Whether Article 18 jurisdiction can constitutionally apply to United States citizens not otherwise subject to the Code is a question that has yet to be decided by the courts. The answer depends primarily on how the courts would view the Article 18 grant of jurisdiction. The courts may determine the jurisdiction is in furtherance of the power of Congress "To make Rules for the Government and Regulation of the land and naval forces."[123] Should the courts adopt this view, Toth and the line of cases that followed would provide strong argument that court-martial jurisdiction under Article 18 does not exist over former servicemen and civilians not otherwise subject to the Code. The Supreme Court decisions limiting court-martial jurisdiction over civilians and former servicemen then would appear to have also restricted

Article 18 jurisdiction to only that which is essential to maintaining the discipline of the armed forces. The language in Toth stating that clause 14 of Article I, § 8, does not allow Congress to extend court-martial jurisdiction over those not "actually members of the armed forces"[124] would seem to confirm the view that Article 18 is only to be used for regulating the armed forces.

On the other hand, the courts may consider Article 18 as deriving from the war powers of Congress and its power to punish "Offenses against the Law of Nations."[125] Should this view prevail, it can persuasively be argued that Article 18 is a recognition by Congress of the existence of the law of war and the common-law military commission. The jurisdiction provided by Article 18 then would be considered a statutory alternative to the common-law military commission for law of war violations. Nothing contrary to this view is contained in the language of Article 21 which precludes Article 18 court-martial jurisdiction from being exclusive in law of war cases that also are punishable by military commission.[126]

The Court of Military Appeals decision in Averette raises the issue of when Article 18 jurisdiction can apply to civilians. In Averette, the court held the words "in time of war" meant only a war declared by Congress in regard to Article 2(10) of the Code.[127] The court acknowledged it had, in other decisions, held the words "in time of war" to apply to conflicts other than a declared war. The decisions were distinguished as not involving the "constitutionally delicate question of military jurisdiction over civilians."[128] The *Averette* decision holds in effect that the term "in time of war" will continue to mean most any armed conflict in regard to military offenders, but will mean only a declared war in regard to extending Article 2(10) court-martial jurisdiction over civilians. Should the courts extend the *Averette* holding to Article 18, court-martial jurisdiction over civilians for violations of the law of war then would exist only in time of declared war.

However, the better view is that Article 18 establishes court-martial jurisdiction over all persons for violations of the law of war regardless of the nature of the conflict. This view prevails if Article 18 jurisdiction is considered the same as that of the common-law military commission. The plain meaning of the words of Article 18 certainly supports this position. The law of war applies to both declared and undeclared wars. Therefore, military commissions and general courts-martial should have jurisdiction over all war crimes and war criminals. Article 18 jurisdiction, unlike the jurisdiction invoked by Article 2(10), should not pertain to the maintaining of discipline and order within the armed forces. The source of Article 18 jurisdiction should rather be considered as deriving from the war powers of Congress and the power of Congress to punish violators of the law of war.

The question of the source and extent of Article 18 jurisdiction will not be answered by the courts until such time as the military authorities attempt to prosecute someone under this provision. Therefore, in cases of war crimes committed by persons not otherwise subject to the Code, use of the military commission would appear to be the safest way to proceed at this time.

It should be noted, however, while the military commission may provide an acceptable court for the purpose of trying those charged with war crimes, the majority of the offenders affected by the Averette and Toth decisions will be persons charged with violations of the punitive articles of the Code which do not constitute war crimes. For those individuals the lack of criminal jurisdiction which presently exists will continue to provide a means to avoid the law.

IV. Regaining Jurisdiction

More than twenty years have elapsed since the Supreme Court found court-martial jurisdiction over former servicemen to be unconstitutional. It has been over fifteen years since Article 2(11) jurisdiction over civilians accompanying the armed forces was held unconstitutional. Only Congressional legislation can again extend criminal jurisdiction to these two classes of defendants. Although there have been a number of legislative proposals during this long period of time, Congress has not been able to enact legislation that would re-establish the lost criminal jurisdiction. The Criminal Justice Reform Act of 1975 is presently the best vehicle for regaining the criminal jurisdiction once possessed by the Uniform Code. In analyzing the extra-territorial provisions of the Act, it is helpful to look at some of the early ideas for re-establishing the disapproved jurisdiction of Articles 2(11) and 3(a).

A. Early Proposals

Recommendations and suggestions for regaining the lost jurisdiction began with the very Supreme Court decisions which narrowed court-martial jurisdiction over civilians. In his opinion in Toth, Justice Black states that Congress had the constitutional power to provide for federal district court jurisdiction of discharged servicemen accused of committing offenses while on active duty.[129] In addition, he stated that federal jurisdiction over former servicemen was suggested by the Judge Advocate General of the Army during Congressional hearings concerning Article 3(a) of the Code.[130] Similarly, Justice Frankfurter, in his concurring opinion in Covert, concluded that Congress has the power to provide for trial and punishment of civilian dependents accompanying the armed forces overseas should it find military discipline to be seriously affected by civilian defendants being able to commit capital offenses without being punished.[131]

Justice Clark in McElroy offered other solutions. One suggestion was that civilian employees of the armed forces be required to agree in writing to submit to court-martial jurisdiction.[132] He noted that the Supreme Court in 1897 had approved such an arrangement in the case of civilian paymaster's clerks aboard Navy ships.[133] A second suggestion by Justice Clark was that civilian employees of the armed forces stationed outside the United States be either inducted or enlisted in the armed forces.[134] Additionally, others have suggested that Congress provide for the trial of civilian employees and dependands accused of committing petty offenses overseas by a United States Commissioner's Court.[135]

In 1962 the Senate Subcommittee on Constitutional Rights held hearings during which information concerning the lack of jurisdiction and recommendations to correct the problem were obtained. Information provided to the Subcommittee by the Department of the Army included draft legislation which would have granted federal district courts jurisdiction over serious offenses committed overseas by United States citizens and other persons owing allegiance to the United States. The legislative proposals would have re-established jurisdiction over those formerly covered by Article 2(11) of the

Code. The draft legislation, in addition, would have vested
federal district courts with jurisdiction over former
servicemen charged with committing serious offenses while
on active duty.[136] The Department of the Navy previously
had favored a Department of Defense proposal for a constitutional amendment authorizing court-martial jurisdiction
over persons who had previously been covered by Article 2(11)
of the Code.[137]

In 1966 joint hearings were held concerning legislation
to improve military justice.[138] Two of the bills considered
would have vested jurisdiction over military employees,
dependents and former servicemembers in federal district
courts.[139] Suggestions presented during the hearings
included expanding the special maritime and territorial
jurisdiction of the United States[140] to include areas where
civilians were accompanying the armed forces, or to all
areas where any United States citizens are present.

In a further attempt to deal with the continuing lack
of jurisdiction, Senator Ervin introduced two bills in 1971.
The first provided for federal district court jurisdiction
over any person who, while subject to the Uniform Code
committed an offense punishable by five years or more
confinement and who was not then subject to the Code.[141]
The second bill would have amended Title 18 of the United
States Code by treating offenses by United States citizens

employed by or accompanying the armed forces overseas, including dependents, as if they had occurred within the special maritime and territorial jurisdiction of the United States.[142]

During the previous year legislation had been introduced which contained somewhat similar provisions. The bill subjected United States citizens who were either in the armed forces or serving with, employed by or accompanying the armed forces overseas subject to the same penalities as if the offenses had occurred within the special maritime and territorial jurisdiction of the United States.[143] Later in the same year a somewhat restricted version of the same legislation was introduced. It limited the offenses covered to those committed while in the performance of official duties, those within an armed forces installation or area of operations of a unit in the field, or those directed against another member of the class of persons covered by the bill.[144]

These examples of proposed legislation demonstrate a continuing desire on the part of some members of Congress to provide a remedy for the constitutional defects in the Code. None of the proposed legislation in this area has succeeded and the lack of jurisdiction over civilians accompanying the armed forces overseas and over former servicemen continues. Recent legislation, however, offers more promise of establishing necessary criminal jurisdiction over these civilians and former servicemen.

B. The Criminal Justice Reform Act of 1975

Legislation is now before Congress which, if enacted, will establish federal jurisdiction over many offenses committed by United States citizens in foreign countries. The proposed legislation is entitled the "Criminal Justice Reform Act of 1975" and was introduced as S. 1 in the Senate in January 1975[145] and as H.R. 3907 in the House of Representatives in February 1975.[146] The purpose of the proposed legislation is to revise and reform Title 18 of the United States Code into a new federal criminal code. Section 204 of the proposed Act is entitled "Extraterritorial Jurisdiction of the United States" and is intended to extend the criminal jurisdiction of the United States outside of the general jurisdiction of the United States in certain situations.[147]

Should Section 204 of the Act become law, it would not be the Nation's first experience with extraterritorial jurisdiction. The United States has used consular courts for both civil and criminal trials, including capital cases. The best known example of consular court jurisdiction is Ross v. McIntyre.[148] In Ross the Supreme Court approved the murder conviction of a seaman on an American vessel in Japanese waters.[149] Various Congressional enactments and treaties previously have provided criminal jurisdiction over United States citizens by counsels at various times in our history in such places as Japan, Borneo, Madagascar, Korea, the Congo, Ethiopia, Persia, Samoa, Siam, Tonga Islands, Tripoli and Morocco.[150] Not until 1956 did the United States relinquish consular jurisdiction in Morocco.[151] The counsels had the power to initiate charges, arrest, try, convict and punish offenders.

In 1906 Congress provided for the establishment of a United States Court for China which sat in various Chinese cities where American communities existed..[152] The court was legislated out of existence in 1948 pursuant to a treaty between China and the United States.[153] During its existence the Court for China adjudicated numerous civil and criminal cases. Criminal convictions by the court have been upheld by United States District Courts and the United States Court of Appeals as recently as 1942.[154] The defendants convicted by the consular courts or the United States Court for China were not accorded the rights of indictment by grand jury or trial by jury, the lack of which in courts-martial have been found so objectionable by some. The lack of indictment or trial by jury was also the approved practice in the Insular Cases.[155]

Additionally, certain federal crimes have been held to apply extraterritorially if Congress so intended. One example of the courts finding such Congressional intent is the decision of Kawakita v. United States.[156] In Kawakita the Supreme

46

Court found that the applicable statute was intended to apply extraterritorially to the offense of treason committed in Japan.[157]

Many of the past means of exercising extraterritorial jurisdiction are no longer politically or judicially acceptable. However, the continued presence of large numbers of American citizens outside the general jurisdiction of the United States makes new legislation necessary. Section 204 of the Act is the latest attempt on the part of Congress to deal with the old problem of extraterritorial jurisdiction.

Section 204 contains nine categories of extraterritorial offenses. Subsections (a) through (f) cover such crimes as treason, counterfeiting of United States currency or stamps, fraud against the United States and distribution of drugs for sale within the United States.[158] The subsections primarily apply extraterritorial jurisdiction to offenses involving federal functions.

Subsection (h) provides jurisdiction where "the offense is committed by or against a national of the United States at a place outside the jurisdiction of any nation."[159] This provision will provide an appropriate remedy for offenses which occur in such geographical locations as Antarctica.[160] Another example of its possible application is demonstrated by the recent prosecution of a United States citizen for the homocide of a fellow employee at a research station located on an ice island in the Artic Ocean.[161]

Subsection (g) of Section 204 is the provision that remedies the lack of United States jurisdiction over civilians in close proximity to our military forces and is, therefore, the provision that is of most interest to military commanders and their judge advocates. It provides that

> "...an offense is committed within the extraterritorial jurisdiction of the United States if it is committed outside the general jurisdiction of the United States and:...
> "(g) the offense is committed by a federal public servant other than a member of the armed forces who is subject to court-martial jurisdiction for the offense, who is outside the United States because of his official duties, or by a member of his household residing abroad because of such public servant's official duties, or by a person accompanying the military forces of the United States.[162]

The effect of Subsection (g) is to extend the federal criminal code to federal employees performing duties outside the United States, to dependents of federal employees residing abroad, and to persons accompanying the armed forces in foreign countries. Excluded from this extension of the federal criminal code are members of the armed forces who commit offenses punishable by the Uniform Code.

Subsection (g) will close the gap created by the loss of Article 2(11) court-martial jurisdiction by extending federal jurisdiction to those employed by the Department of Defense or other government agencies overseas and to those civilians serving with or accompanying the armed forces overseas. Therefore, when this portion of the Act becomes law, peacetime jurisdiction by the United States over such persons will be re-established.

Subsection (g) is also intended to apply to discharged servicemen who have committed offenses overseas while on active duty, but who are no longer subject to the Uniform Code of Military Justice as a result of the Toth decision. While the language used is somewhat unclear, it can be understood to mean that jurisdiction attaches to a former member of the armed forces if he is no longer subject to court-martial jurisdiction for the offense. This interpretation is reached if the phrase "other than a member of the armed forces who is subject to court-martial jurisdiction for the offense"[163] is construed to mean that federal jurisdiction is excluded where a serviceman remains subject to court-martial jurisdiction for the offense.[164]

Subsection (g) of course will not restore completely pre-Toth jurisdiction because a former serviceman could still not be prosecuted for certain offenses under the Uniform Code of Military Justice that are peculiar to members of the military and for which a former serviceman could have been prosecuted under Article 3(a) of the Code. The trial of purely military offenses by federal district court has been suggested in the past and has been provided for in some previously proposed legislation. This is a matter of minor importance and it is difficult to see how the inability to bring former servicemen to account for purely military offenses committed on active duty could have any significant impact on the good order and discipline of the armed forces.

Should Subsection (g) be enacted, it will close the Toth-created gap to the extent that other than purely military offenses will be punishable by federal law as if they had occurred within the territorial jurisdiction of the United States. The former serviceman who commits an offense overseas will then be amenable to the same federal criminal sanctions as one who commits the same offense within the United States. Subsection (g) of the proposed legislation will comply substantially with the recommendations of the Judge Advocate General of the Army concerning Article 3(a) during Senate hearings on the Code[165] and the suggestions for a remedy put forth by the Supreme Court in the Toth decision.[166]

The issue of who is to exercise jurisdiction in time of war pursuant to Article 2(10), however, is not addressed in the bill. Inasmuch as Subsection (g) does not differentiate between time of peace or time of war, there is no reason to believe that it is intended to apply only in time of peace. Article 2(10) of the Code, as interpreted by the Court of Military Appeals in the Averette decision, still provides for court-martial jurisdiction over those serving with or accompanying the armed forces in the field in time of declared war.[167] Section 205 of the Act sheds some light in this area, although it also raises further questions.

Section 205 provides that federal jurisdiction is not

preemptive in three situations. The last of these situations

specifies that unless expressly provided otherwise, federal

jurisdiction over an offense will not preclude

> a court-martial, military commission, court of inquiry,
> provost court, or other military court of the United
> States from exercising its jurisdiction to enforce
> the law applicable to the conduct involved pursuant
> to the Uniform Code of Military Justice..., any other
> federal statute, or the law of war.[168]

By viewing Section 205(a)(3) and Section 204(g) together

it is apparent that if court-martial jurisdiction exists

under Article 2(10) of the Code and federal jurisdiction

exists under Section 204(g) of the Act, federal jurisdiction

would not be preemptive of the court-martial jurisdiction

and both would exist concurrently.

Concurrent jurisdiction raises the issue of which agency

should take jurisdiction of the offense. Because Article 2(10)

now only applies to time of declared war, it can be assumed

from the nature of warfare today that the military situation

in a declared war would be serious in most places where

military forces were operating in the field. The virtually

uncontested military control of the air and of the sea that

Americans have been accustomed to since World War II might

well not exist. Additionally, civilian witnesses in a combat

area can become very difficult to locate as the military

situations changes. In addition, witnesses in a combat zone

often require hospitalization or die from disease or wounds.

These are factors that rarely occur to a civilian attorney, but are only too well known to judge advocates who have prosecuted or defended cases where the armed forces have been committed in a combat role. Judge Sibley of the United States District Court for the Northern District of Georgia acknowledged the difficulty of litigation under these circumstances in the following manner:

> The rapid movement of soldiers, causing the scattering of witnesses before the civil courts could act, as well as the necessity of firm discipline and full control over an army when on a war footing, are prime causes for the substitution of courts-martial for civil courts in time of war.[169]

Under the conditions described, the military authorities would be in the best position to exercise jurisdiction. Additionally, the effective prosecution in the federal courts in most cases arising in a combat zone would be virtually impossible.

One problem with using Article 2(10) jurisdiction, however, is the tendency of the federal courts to allow civilians much greater latitude in the collateral attack of court-martial proceedings on jurisdictional grounds. Federal courts in the past often have acted on a habeas corpus petition filed by a civilian defendant in a court-martial before his remedies in the military justice system have been exhausted. The rationale of the courts has been that it would be unfair to allow the disruption of a civilian's life and the deprivation of a civilian's liberty during the time it would take a defendant to exhaust his military remedies. The requirement of a military defendant to exhaust his remedies prior to filing a habeas corpus petition was distinguished by the Supreme Court in Noyd v. Bond.[170] The Court, in a footnote, provided its rationale for approving the different treatment of military and civilian defendants as follows:

> We did so, however, because we did not believe that the expertise of military courts extended to the consideration of constitutional claims of the type presented. Moreover, it appeared especially unfair to require exhaustion of military remedies when the complainants raised substantial arguments denying the right of the military to try them at all.[171]

In 1975 the Supreme Court in Schlesinger v. Councilman[172] noted the above language in Noyd and indicated by dictum that where a civilian defendant in a court-martial raised a jurisdictional issue, exhaustion of remedies would not be required.[173] It is clear, therefore, that a collateral attack by habeas corpus petition of a prosecution pursuant to Article 2(10) would be acted upon by the federal courts and litigation concerning the matter would develop in the United States.

Section 205 of the Act also leaves intact military commission jurisdiction which may exist pursuant to the Uniform Code of Military Justice, any other federal statute, or the law of war. The result is concurrent jurisdiction between the federal courts and the courts of a military government in territory occupied by our armed forces. Occupation courts have a history of handling large numbers of cases and,

as in Madsen, are often composed of civilian judges.[174]
In an occupied area military commissions or occupation
courts are better able to handle most cases in which they have
jurisdiction than are the federal courts located in the
United States.

Concurrent jurisdiction also will exist in the area of
war crimes. Jurisdiction over servicemen remains exclusively
with the military courts because of the Article 18 grant of
jurisdiction over war crimes and the excluding clause of Section
204(g) of the Act. Exclusive jurisdiction over a serviceman
also would remain with the military courts should an offense be
charged as violation of one of the punitive articles of the
Code rather than as a war crime.

However, in the case of a civilian charged with a war crime,
the possibility of court-martial jurisdiction pursuant to
Article 18 of the Code would not preclude jurisdiction in the
federal courts. The reservation of court-martial jurisdiction
contained in Section 204(g) pertains only to members of the
armed forces. Federal jurisdiction also would extend to former
servicemen should the language of Section 204(g) be construed
to include those who were subject to the Code at the time of
the offense, but who are no longer members of the armed forces.
The status of the defendant, as either a present member
or not a member of the armed forces, would determine
whether the federal courts have jurisdiction under
Section 204(g). Prosecution of a civilian or former

serviceman accused of a war crime could proceed in the federal courts if the offense was also a violation of the federal penal code. In addition, the offense could be prosecuted as a war crime either by a general court-martial pursuant to Article 18 of the Code or by a military commission.

An additional means of prosecuting war crimes in the federal courts is provided by Section 204(i) which provides that a crime is committed when

> "(i) the offense is comprehended by the genaric terms
> of, and is committed under circumstances specified by,
> a treaty or other international agreement, to which
> the United States is a party, that provides for, or
> requires the United States to provide for, federal
> jurisdiction over such offense."[175]

In other words Section 204(i) establishes federal jurisdiction over offenses defined by treaty or agreement to which the United States is a party when the agreement also requires the United States to provide for such jurisdiction. The provision would apply, for example, to the four Geneva Conventions for the Protection of War Victims. The Geneva Conventions specifically require the High Contracting Parties to enact the legislation necessary to provide penal sanctions for those who commit, or order to commit, grave breaches of the Conventions.[176] Section 204(i), in conjunction with the Geneva Conventions, creates federal jurisdiction over any person, civilian or military, who commits an act which constitutes a grave breach of one of the Conventions.

The jurisdiction created by Section 204(i) applies to

both civilians and members of the armed forces since the reservation of exclusive court-martial jurisdiction over servicemen appears only in Section 204(g). Federal jurisdiction under Section 204(i) is not exclusive, however, because Section 205(a)(3) precludes federal jurisdiction from preempting any existing court-martial or military commission jurisdiction.

As can be seen, there will exist under the Uniform Code and the Reform Act various means of prosecuting individuals for offenses that constitute war crimes. In the case of a serviceman, prosecution could conceivably be pursued by court-martial as a violation of one of the punitive articles of the Code; by general court-martial pursuant to Article 18 of the Code; by military commission; or in the federal courts pursuant to Section 204(i) if the offense is covered by an appropriate treaty or international agreement. As for a civilian or a former serviceman, prosecution could occur by general court-martial pursuant to Article 18; by military commission; in a federal court pursuant to Section 204(g) if the offense constitutes a violation of the federal penal code; or in a federal court pursuant to Section 204(i) if the offense is covered by an appropriate treaty or international agreement.

One of the disadvantages to using the federal courts to prosecute offenses occuring outside of the United States is the obtaining of witnesses, particularly witnesses who are foreign nationals. Not only will there be great expense in bringing witnesses to the United States, a foreign national may well refuse to appear as a witness. The problems of locating and transporting witnesses in time of war have been mentioned. Even in peacetime prosecutors and defense lawyers will experience great difficulty in obtaining witnesses because federal courts are limited in their ability to subpoena foreign nationals located outside of the general jurisdiction of the United States.[177]

Legislation can do little to assist the courts in compelling foreign nationals to appear as witnesses in the United States. The only practical solution lies in treaties or agreements with other nations. The effect of not being able to obtain the presence of witnesses is to render the extraterritorial jurisdiction provisions of the Act useless in cases where the witnesses are essential.

When necessary foreign witnesses cannot be obtained, another judicial forum will need to be used. The most obvious alternative is the court-martial in cases where jurisdiction under the Code exists. While the court-martial may also lack compulsory process over foreign nationals,[178] it can convene near the location of witnesses who may be reluctant to leave their homes and families. The assistance of local civilian or military officials can also be engaged to obtain witnesses before courts-martial convened in foreign jurisdictions.

V. Recommendations

Section 204 of the Act, as complemented by Section 205, constitutes a viable solution to the problem facing overseas military commanders who presently lack criminal jurisdiction over civilians accompanying the armed forces. Both provisions of the Act are necessary for regaining jurisdiction over civilians in foreign countries while also retaining present military jurisdiction.

A. Recommended Modifications

A change in the wording of Section 204(g) is needed to ensure the obtaining of criminal jurisdiction over offenses committed by former servicemen while serving on active duty. The intent to reserve exclusive court-martial jurisdiction over only present members of the armed forces must be clearly set forth so that the section obtains federal jurisdiction over former members of the armed forces. The intended result can best be accomplished by inserting the word "present" in the exclusion phrase of Section 204(g) and by specifically setting forth that court-martial jurisdiction is only reserved where the offender is subject to the Code at both the time of the offense and at the time charged. The exclusion phrase would then read as follows:

> "(g) the offense is committed by a federal public
> servant other than a <u>present</u> member of the armed forces
> who, <u>at the time of the offense and at the time charged</u>,
> is subject to court-martial jurisdiction for the offense,..."

The recommended language goes further in specifying when court-martial jurisdiction is exclusive than does a change in the wording of this provision contained in a more recent version of the bill introduced in the House.[179] The recommended change would insure federal jurisdiction over former servicemen accused of committing an offense while on active duty overseas. A former serviceman defendant would then be precluded from arguing that federal jurisdiction under Section 204(g) does not apply to him because he committed the offense while a member of the armed forces and while subject to court-martial jurisdiction.

It is further recommended that the same language reserving exclusive court-martial jurisdiction be inserted in Sections 204(h) and 204(i) of the Act. Section 204(h) would then provide

> "(h) the offense is committed by or against a national
> of the United States at a place outside the jurisdiction
> of any nation, <u>other than an offense committed by a present
> member of the armed forces who, at the time of the offense
> and at the time charged, is subject to court-martial
> jurisdiction for the offense.</u>

Section 204(i) would read

> "(i) the offense is comprehended by the generic terms
> of, and is committed under circumstances specified by,
> a treaty or other international agreement, to which the
> United States is a party, that provides for, or requires
> the United States to provide for, federal jurisdiction
> over such offense, <u>other than an offense committed by a
> present member of the armed forces who, at the time of the
> offense and at the time charged, is subject to court-
> martial jurisdiction for the offense.</u>"

The effect of the recommended changes would be to maintain exclusive court-martial jurisdiction over those subject to the Uniform Code who commit offenses defined by these two provisions. The retaining of exclusive court-martial jurisdiction would be consistent with the non-application of O'Callahan overseas[180] by precluding the trial of servicemen in the civilian courts unless the offense is one for which there otherwise exists federal jurisdiction.

B. Recommended Policy in Exercising Jurisdiction

Enactment of the Reform Act will result in the existence of both military and federal jurisdiction over civilians accompanying the armed forces in time of war or occupation. Commanders and their judge advocates will need guidance as to the appropriate procedures to be used in the various circumstances and locations in which cases involving civilians might be expected to arise.

It is recommended that court-martial convening authorities be advised that court-martial jurisdiction under Article 2(10) of the Code continues to exist in time of declared war over persons serving with or accompanying the armed forces in the field. Commanders should be advised that immediately upon the declaration of war by the United States, convening authorities will assert military jurisdiction over all persons and offenses covered by Article 2(10) which occur beyond the

territorial jurisdiction of the United States.[181] Charges
would be preferred by the convening authority and preparations
for trial by court-martial would commence. However, should
concurrent jurisdiction under Article 2(10) and the federal
criminal code exist, a determination would then be required
as to whether the military or civilian authorities should
prosecute. It is recommended that the Department of Justice
make this determination in all such cases based upon the
various factors involved.

Under this policy, once a civilian has been charged by
the military authorities, the Department of Justice would be
notified and recommendations on the matter would be obtained
from the court-martial convening authority and senior military
commanders. The recommendations would indicate the preference
of the convening authority for either military or federal
jurisdiction to be exercised in the case and would include
information as to why trial in the recommended jurisdiction
would be more appropriate. If the Department of Justice
elects to exercise jurisdiction, the case will be turned over
to the appropriate United States Attorney. On the other hand,
if the Department of Justice declines to prosecute, the
convening authority would proceed as in any other court-
martial. An expeditious process of obtaining a decision from
the Department of Justice would be required in order to avoid
speedy trial problems should the military authorities eventually
prosecute the case.

Military exigencies during a declared war, however, may be such that communication between the convening authority and the Department of Justice is impractical or impossible. When this occurs the general court-martial convening authority will be authorized to make the determination that communication cannot be established. He can then either convene a general court-martial or authorize the convening of a lesser court-martial. His decision, of course, would be subject to review by the military appellate courts and possibly in the federal courts if the determination was considered jurisdictional in nature.

Concurrent federal and military commission jurisdiction will also exist over United States citizens in occupied areas. A policy determination by the Executive Branch will be required to determine if the federal courts in the United States or military commissions and occupations courts in the occupied area will exercise jurisdiction. The history of successful use of commissions and occupation courts subsequent to World War II makes their future use likely should the need exist.

The military services must continue to be prepared to establish military commissions in occupied territory as a part of the military government in such areas. Continued updating of civil affairs training and manuals is required to keep abreast of new developments in the law that might have application to the establishment and conducting of military commissions. Additionally, it may be desirable, and in some areas even necessary, that the procedures used by military commissions be refined so as to more resemble those used by the Article III courts or other statutory proceedings.

A more difficult area is the developing of a policy in regard to war crimes. The Department of Defense must develop a positive position on the prosecution of those who commit war crimes. The policy is necessary to prevent individuals who commit war crimes to avoid prosecution as occurred during the Vietnam era.

Different approaches to exercising jurisdiction over different classes of defendants is required. In cases of military personnel who have committed war crimes, the safest and most appropriate means to prosecute is by court-martial for a violation of one of the punitive articles of the Code. If the criminal act does not constitute a violation of a punitive article, then trial by general court-martial for a violation of the law of war pursuant to Article 18 of the Code would be the better alternative. The trial of servicemen by court-martial rather than by military commission or in the civilian courts is more appropriate. There exists no question of Uniform Code jurisdiction over a serviceman and a court-martial can convene wherever the military forces are located. This reduces the problem of obtaining evidence and witnesses. Additionally, a military court is a better trier of fact in cases involving crimes committed in combat by military personnel.

In the case of civilians or former servicemen charged with war crimes, the Executive Branch must maintain its authority and ability to try offenders and must develop a viable policy in this regard. The best policy would be to require the Justice Department to prosecute civilians and former servicemen charged with war crimes in the federal courts if the witnesses and evidence required to do so are available in the United States. Trial by the civilian courts would avoid the unpolular exercise of military jurisdiction over civilians and would guarantee defendants certain constitutional and procedural rights not available in the military courts. However, in cases where the testimony of essential witnesses could only be obtained in foreign countries, the Executive Branch must be prepared to convene military commissions at these locations.

Additionally, the Executive Branch must be prepared to convene military commissions within the United States, or elsewhere if necessary, should a civilian or former serviceman be charged with a war crime over which there is no federal jurisdiction. While general court-martial jurisdiction over civilians charged with violations of the law of war may be possible under Article 18 of the Code, the military commission, with its authority derived from the war powers of Congress and the Executive, is the safest and more accepted way to proceed. By regulating Article 18 jurisdiction to the courts-martial of servicemem only, there is less opportunity to

confront the Judiciary's objections to civilian defendants
being tried by courts-martial.

IV. Conclusion

The time to prepare workable positions and policy is now
because when the need for their application arises, little
time to develop well-thought through through solutions will
exist. The legal resources of the services will have more
than enough to do handling the difficult legal problems that
will be developing on a daily basis. Justice will be better
served if those responsible for carrying it out have an
established policy and procedure to apply rather than being
required to develop policies and procedures on an ad hoc
basis in reaction to fast moving events.

FOOTNOTES

1. Interview of Paul D. Meadlow on the CBS News of November 24, 1969.

2. In re Lo Dolce, 106 F. Supp. 455 (W.D.N.Y. 1952). This case was a proceeding on application by the Italian government for the extradition of Lo Dolce for the homocide of the American officer and a related robbery. The court denied extradition holding that United States military personnel in enemy country are subject only to the laws of "their own government." Id. at 459.

3. Hironimus v. Durant, 168 F. 2d 288 (4th Cir. 1948), cert. denied, 355 U.S. 818 (1948).

4. S. 1, 94th Cong., 1st Sess. (1975) (hereinafter cited as The Criminal Justice Reform Act of 1975). The bill was introduced in the Senate on January 15, 1975. The same act was introduced in the House of Representatives on February 27, 1975, H.R. 3907, 94th Cong., 1st Sess. (1975).

5. United States ex rel. Toth v. Quarles, 350 U.S. 11 (1955).

6. Uniform Code of Military Justice art. 3(a), 10 U.S.C. 803 (a) (1975). Article 3(a) provides

> (a) Subject to section 843 of this title (article 43), no person charged with having committed, while in a status in which he was subject to this chapter, an offense against this chapter, punishable by confinement for five years or more and for which the person cannot be tried in the courts of the United States or of a State, a Territory, or the District of Columbia, may be relieved from amenability to trial by court-martial by reason of the termination of that status.

7. 350 U.S. at 14.

8. Id. at 15.

9. Id. at 23.

10. Reid v. Covert, 354 U.S. 1 (1957).

11. 354 U. S. at 3, 4.

1

12. Uniform Code of Military Justice art. 2(11), 10 U.S.C. § 802 (11) (1975). Article 2(11) provides

    The following persons are subject to this chapter:
    (11) Subject to any treaty or agreement to which the United States is or may be a party or to any accepted rule of international law, persons serving with, employed by, or accompanying the armed forces outside the United States and outside the following: the Canal Zone, Puerto Rico, Guam, and the Virgin Islands.

13. 354 U.S. at 23.

14. Id. at 49 (concurring opinion).

15. Id. at 65 (concurring opinion).

16. Kinsella v. United States ex rel. Singleton, 361 U.S. 234 (1960).

17. Grisham v. Hagan, 361 U.S. 278 (1960).

18. McElroy v. United States ex rel. Guagliardo, 361 U.S. 281.

19. 361 U.S. at 248.

20. Id.

21. 361 U.S. 278.

22. Id. at 280.

23. 361 U.S. 281.

24. Id. (a companion case).

25. Id. at 283.

26. United States v. Averette, 19 U.S.C.M.A. 363, 41 C.M.R. 363 (1970).

27. Uniform Code of Military Justice art. 2(10), 10 U.S.C. § 802 (10) (1975).

28. 19 U.S.C.M.A. at 365, 41 C.M.R. at 365.

29. Id.

30. Id. at 366, 41 C.M.R. at 366.

31. See Note, _Military Law--"In Time of War" Under the Uniform Code of Military Justice: An Elusive Standard_, 67 MICH. L. REV. 841, 845, 846 (1969).

32. _Id.._ at 848 n.56; See 95 Cong Rec. 5718 (1949); 96 Cong. Rec. 1412 (1950).

33. 19 U.S.C.M.A. at 365, 41 C.M.R. at 365.

34. United States v. Anderson, 17 U.S.C.M.A. 588, 38 C.M.R. 386 (1968).

35. 19 U.S.C.M.A. at 365, 41 C.M.R. at 365.

36. Zamora v. Woodson, 19 U.S.C.M.A. 403, 42 C.M.R. 5 (1970).

37. _Id._ at 404, 42 C.M.R. at 6.

38. _Id._

39. _Id._

40. Robb v. United States, 456 F. 2d 768 (Ct. Cl. 1972).

41. _Id._ at 771.

42. _Id._ at 772.

43. Latney v. Ignatius, 416 F. 2d 821 (D.C. Cir. 1969).

44. O'Callahan v. Parker, 395 U.S. 258 (1969). The Court held that for military jurisdiction to exist over a serviceman the offense must be "service connected." _Id._ at 272.

45. 416 F. 2d at 283.

46. _Id._

47. 19 U.S.C.M.A. at 364, 41 C.M.R. at 364.

48. _Id._

49. _Id._ at 364, 365.

50. _Id._ at 365.

51. Reid v. Covert, 354 U.S. at 33, 33 n.59.

52. _Id._ at 33.

53. <u>Id</u>. at 34 n.61.

54. 361 U.S. at 284.

55. <u>See</u> Perlstein v. United States, 151 F. 2d 167 (3rd Cir.
    1945), <u>cert. granted</u>, 327 U.S. 777 (1946), <u>cert. dismissed</u>,
    328 U.S. 822 (1946); Hines v. Mikell, 259 F. 28 (4th
    Cir 1919); <u>Ex parte</u> Jochen 257 F. 200 (S.C.Tex. 1919);
    <u>Ex parte Falls</u>, 251 F. 415 (D.N.J. 1918); <u>Ex parte</u>
    Gerlach, 247 F. 616 (S.D.N.Y. 1917); Shilman v. United
    States, 73 Supp. 648, <u>rev'd in part</u>, 164 F. 2d 649
    (2nd Cir. 1947), <u>cert. denied</u>, 333 U.S. 837 (1948);
    <u>In re</u> Berue, 54 F. Supp. 252 (S.D.Ohio 1944); McCune v.
    Kilpatrick, 53 F. Supp. 80 (E.D.Va. 1943); <u>In re</u> DiBartolo,
    50 F. Supp. 929 (S.D.N.Y. 1943). as cited in Reid v.
    Covert, 354 U.S. at 33 n.59.

56. W. WINTHROP, MILITARY LAW AND PRECEDENTS 832-833 (2d
    ed. 1920 reprint) (hereinafter cited as WINTHROP).

57.   The Congress shall have Power to...provide for the
            Common Defense...; To declare War, grant Letters of
            Marque and Reprisal, and make Rules concerning
            Captures on Land and Water; To raise and support
            Armies...; To provide and maintain a Navy; To
            make Rules for the Government and Regulation of the
            land and naval Forces; ...To provide for calling
            forth the Militia to execute the Laws of the Union,
            suppress Insurections and repel Invasions; To
            provide for organizing, arming, and disciplining,
            the Militia, and for governing such Part of them as
            may be employed in the Service of the United States...

    U.S. CONST. art. I, § 8, cls 1, 11-16.

58. "To define and punish Piracies and Felonies committed on
    the high Seas, and Offenses against the Law of Nations,..."
    U.S. CONST. art. I, § 8, cl 10.

59.   The President shall be Commander in Chief of the Army
            and Navy of the United States, and of the Militia
            of the several States, when called into the actual
            Service of the United States; ...

    U.S. CONST. art. II, § 2.

60. WINTHROP, <u>supra</u> note 56, at 831. <u>See</u> Madsen v. Kinsella,
    343 U.S. at 346 n.9.

61. Madsen v. Kinsella, 343 U.S. at 347 n.10.

4

62. _Ex parte_ Quirin v. Cox, 317 U.S. 1 (1942)

63. _In re_ Yamashita v. Styer, 327 U.S. 1 (1945).

64. 317 U.S. at 26.

65. _Id._ at 27.

66. _Id._

67. _Id._ at 44.

68. _Id._

69. _Id._ at 46.

70. _Id._

71. 327 U.S. 1.

72. _Id._ at 13, 14.

73. _Id._ at 6.

74. _Id._ at 8.

75. _Id._

76. _Id._ at 7.

77. _Id._ at 12.

78. _Id._

79. _Id._ at 20.

80. _Id._

81. Johnson v. Eisentrager, 339 U.S. 763 (1950).

82. Id. at 786.

83. Id. at 766.

84. _Id._ at 768.

85. Madsen v. Kinsella, 343 U.S. 341 (1952).

86. _Id._ at 348.

87. _Id._

88. Id. at 354.

89. Id. at 348 n.13.

90. Id. at 357, 358.

91. Id. at 362.

92. Id. at 345.

93. Reid v. Covert, 354 U.S. at 81 (dissenting opinion).

94. Id. at 21.

95. Id.

96. Id. at 35 n.63.

97. Id.

98. 361 U.S. 281.

99. Id. at 283 n.2.

100. Rose v. McNamara, 357 F. 2d 924 (D.C. Cir. 1967).

101. Id. at 926.

102. Id. n.4.

103. Id. at 929.

104. Id.

105. U.S. v. Calley, 46 C.M.R. 1131 (ACMR 1973) The Court
     noted that "(a)lthough all charges could have been laid
     as war crimes, they were prosecuted under the UCMJ."
     Id. at 1138.

106. WINTHROP, supra note 56 at 838.

107. Uniform Code of Military Justice art. 18, 10 U.S.C.
     § 818 (1975).

108. Uniform Code of Military Justice art. 21, 10 U.S.C.
     § 821 (1975).

109. 1949 Geneva Convention for the Amelioration of the Con-
     dition of the Wounded and Sick in Armed Forces in the Field
     (1955), 6 U.S.T. 3114, T.I.A.S. No. 3362 (hereinafter cited

as Sick and Wounded Convention; 1949 Geneva Convention for the Amelioration of the Condition of Wounded, Sick and Shipwrecked Members of Armed Forces at Sea (1955), 6 U.S.T. 3217, T.I.A.S. No. 3363 (hereinafter cited as Shipwrecked Convention; 1949 Geneva Convention Relative to the Treatment of Prisoners of War (1955) 6 U.S.T. 3316, T.I.A.S. No. 3364 (hereinafter cited as Prisoner of War Convention); 1949 Geneva Convention Relative to to the Protection of Civilian Persons in Time of War (1955), 6 U.S.T. 3516, T.I.A.S. No. 3365 (hereinafter cited as Civilian Persons Convention).

110. Art. 49 of Sick and Wounded Convention; Art. 50 of Shipwrecked Convention; Art. 129 of Prisoner of War Convention; Art. 146 of Civilian Persons Convention.

111. Art. 49 of Sick and Wounded Convention; Art. 50 of Shipwrecked Convention; Art. 129 of Prisoner of War Convention; Art. 146 of Civilian Persons Convention.

112. 55 U.N. ECOSOC, Supp. 1, at 25, 26, U.N. Dec. E/2508 (1973).

113. Art. 49 of Sick and Wounded Convention; Art. 50 of Shipwrecked Convention; Art. 129 of Prisoner of War Convention; Art. 146 of Civilian Persons Convention.

114. Uniform Code of Military Justice art. 18, 10 U.S.C. § 818 (1975).

115. Art. 2 of Prisoner of War Convention. Article 2 is common to all of the 1949 Geneva Convention. It provides, in part,

> ...the present Convention shall apply to all cases of declared war or of any other armed conflict which may arise between two or more of the High Contracting Parties, even if the state of war is not recognized by one of them.

116. WINTHROP, supra note 56, at 833-834.

117. 317 U.S. 37.

118. Id.

119. Colepaugh v. Looney, 235 F. 2d 429 (10th Cir. 1956).

120. Id. at 432.

121. U.S. CONST. art. I, § 8.

122. 350 U.S. at 13, 14 n.4.

123. U.S. CONST. art. I, § 8.

124. 350 U.S. at 15.

125. U.S. CONST. art I, § 8.

126. Uniform Code of Military Justice art. 21, 10 U.S.C.
     § 821 (1975). Article 21 provides

     > The provisions of this chpater conferring juris-
     > diction upon courts-martial do not deprive military
     > commissions, provost courts, or other military
     > tribunals of concurrent jurisdiction with respect
     > to offenders or offenses that by statute or by
     > the law of war may be tried by military commissions,
     > provost courts, or other military tribunals.

127. 19 U.S.C.M.A. at 365, 41 C.M.R. at 365.

128. Id.

129. 350 U.S. at 20, 21.

130. Id.

131. 351 U.S. at 47.

132. 361 U.S. at 286.

133. Ex parte Reed, 100 U.S. 13 (1879).

134. 361 U.S. at 286.

135. Ehrenhaft, Policing Civilians Accompanying the United
     States Armed Forces Overseas: Can United States
     Commissioners Fill the Jurisdictional Gap?, 36
     GEO. WASH. L. REV. 273 91967).

136. Hearings on Constitutional Rights of Military Personnel
     before the Subcomm. on Constitutional Rights of the
     Senate Comm. on the Judiciary, 87th Cong., 2d Sess. (1962).

137. Id. at 910.

138. Joint Hearings on Bills to Improve the Administration
     of Justice in the Armed Services before the Subcomm. on
     Constitutional Rights of the Senate Comm. on the Judiciary

and a Special Subcomm. of the Senate Comm. on Armed Services, 89th Cong., 2d Sess. (1966).

139. S. 761, 89th Cong., 2nd Sess. (1966); S. 762, 89th Cong., 2d Sess. (1966).

140. See 18 U.S.C. § 7 (1952). For a recent decision holding that an American embassy in a foreign country is within the special maritime and territorial jurisdiction of the United States see U.S. v. Erdos, 474 F. 2d 157 (4th Cir. 1973).

141. S. 1744, 92nd Cong., 1st Sess. (1971)

142. S. 1745, 92nd Cong., 1st Sess. (1971).

143. H.R. 18548, 91st Cong., 2nd Sess. (1970).

144. H.R. 18857, 91st Cong., 2nd Sess. (1970).

145. The Criminal Justice Reform Act of 1975, supra note 4.

146. Id.

147. The Criminal Justice Reform Act of 1975, § 204.

148. Ross v. McIntyre, 140 U.S. 453 (1891).

149. Id. at 480.

150. Reid v. Covert, 354 U.S. at 61, 62.

151. Id. at 62 n.9.

152. Act of June 30, 1906, ch. 3934, 34 Stat. 814.

153. Act of June 25, 1948, ch. 646, 62 Stat. 992; Treaty with the Republic of China, Jan. 11, 1943, 57 Stat., pt. 2, 767 (1943), T.S. No. 984.

154. See Husar v. United States, 26 F. 2d 847 (9th Cir. 1928); Casement v. Squier, 46 F. Supp. 296 (W.D.Wash. 1942).

155. Downes v. Bidwell, 182 U.S. 244 (1901); The Insular cases concerned territories which were acquired, by conquest or otherwise, and where there existed cultures and societies very different from that in the United States. Consequently the Supreme Court found that certain constitutional rights should not apply in these areas. Hawaii v. Mankich, 190 U.S. 197 (1903); Dorr v. United States, 195 U.S. 138 (1904); Balzac v. Puerto Rico, 258 U.S. 298 (1922).

156. Ka--kita v. United States, 343 U.S. 717 (1952).

157. Id. at 733.

158. The Criminal Justice Reform Act of 1975, § 204 (a)-(f).

159. Id. § 204 (h).

160. See generally Bilder, Control of Criminal Conduct in Antarctica, 52 VA. L. REV. 231 (1966).

161. United States v. Escamilla, 467 F. 2d 341 (4th Dir. 1972). The in banc Court of Appeals was equally divided on the issue of whether the district court erred in its ruling that the special maritime and territorial jurisdiction of the United States extended to a crime committed on an unclaimed ice island in the Arctic Ocean. The conviction was reversed on other grounds. Id., at 343.

162 The Criminal Justice Reform Act of 1975, § 204 (g).

163. Id.

164. The reservation of exclusive court-martial jurisdiction can also be construed to mean that no federal jurisdiction exists under Section 204 (g) when the offense was committed by a member of the armed forces who was subject to the Uniform Code at the time of the offense. This interpretation does not consider the status of the accused at the time he was charged with the offense. Under this view neither court-martial jurisdiction nor federal jurisdiction under Section 204 (g) would exist in the case of a former serviceman charged with committing an offense while on active duty. The jurisdictional gap created by Toth, therefore, would continue to exist.

165. Toth v. Quarles, 350 U.S. at 21.

166. 350 U.S. at 20, 21.

167. 19 U.S.C.M.A. at 364; 365, 41 C.M.R. at 364, 365.

168. The Criminal Justice Reform Act of 1975, § 205 (a) (3).

169. Ex parte Givins, 262 F. 702 (N.D.Ga. 1920) at 705.

170. Noyd v. Bond, 395 U.S. 683 (1969).

171. Id. at 696 n.8.

172. Schlesinger v. Councilman, 420 U.S. 738 (1975).

173. <u>Id</u>. at 759.

174. 343 U.S. at 358, n.23.

175. The Criminal Justice Reform Act of 1975, § 204 (i).

176. Art. 49 of Sick and Wounded Convention; Art. 50 of Shipwrecked Convention; Art. 129 of Prisoner of War Convention; Art. 146 of Civilian Persons Convention.

177. <u>See</u> Gillars v. U.S., 182 F. 2d 962 (D.C. Cir. 1950); <u>U.S.</u> v. Haim, 218 F. Supp. 922 (S.D.N.Y. 1963).

178. Uniform Code of Military Justice art. 46, 10 U.S.C. § 846 (1975).

179. H.R. 10850, 94th Cong., 1st Sess. (1975). Section 204 (7) provides for federal jurisdiction if

> The offense is committed by a Federal public servant, other than a member of the armed forces, who at the time charged, is subject to court-martial jurisdiction for the offense,...

180. <u>See</u> U.S. v. Keaton, 19 U.S.C.M.A. 64, 41 C.M.R. 64 (1969). The court in this case held "that the constitutional limitation on court-martial jurisdiction laid down in <u>O'Callahan</u>...is inapplicable to courts-martial held outside the territorial limits of the United States." <u>Id</u>. at 68, 41 C.M.R. at 68.

181. The question of exercising Article 2(10) jurisdiction within the United States is beyond the purview of this article.

182. For a discussion of procedures to be used by military commissions, see Shaneyfelt, <u>War Crimes and the Jurisdictional Maze</u>, 4 INT'L LAW. 924, 931, 933 (1970); U.S. DEP'T OF ARMY, FIELD MANUAL 41-10, CIVIL AFFAIRS OPERATIONS (1967); U.S. DEP'T OF ARMY, FIELD MANUAL 41-5, JOINT MANUAL FOR CIVIL AFFAIRS (1966).